Dear Barbara,

I love your Smile!

Keep Smiling!

Regards

DK Sidhu.

01-27-2021.

MIND CHISELING IN MY GRIEF

By

Dr. Hema Kaur Sidhu

5216 Lynngate Road Columbia, MD 21044
443-851-6395
Sidadoc@gmail.com

ISBN-13: 978-1-4566-3455-1

Acknowledgement

ਆਸਾ ਮਹਲਾ ੪ ॥
Aasaa Mehalaa 4 ||
Aasaa, Fourth Mehl:
ਸੋਪੁਰਖੁ ਆਸਾ (ਮਃ ੪) ਗੁਰੂ ਗ੍ਰੰਥ ਸਾਹਿਬ ਅੰਗ ੧੧

ਤੂੰ ਕਰਤਾ ਸਚਿਆਰੁ ਮੈਡਾ ਸਾਂਈ ॥
Thoon Karathaa Sachiaar Maiddaa Saanee ||
You are the True Creator, my Lord and Master.

ਜੋ ਤਉ ਭਾਵੈ ਸੋਈ ਥੀਸੀ ਜੋ ਤੂੰ ਦੇਹਿ ਸੋਈ ਹਉ ਪਾਈ ॥੧॥ ਰਹਾਉ ॥
Jo Tho Bhaavai Soee Thheesee Jo Thoon Dhaehi Soee Ho Paaee ||1|| Rehaao ||
Whatever pleases You comes to pass. As You give, so do we receive. ||1||Pause||
ਸੋਪੁਰਖੁ ਆਸਾ (ਮਃ ੪) (੨) ੧:੨ - ਗੁਰੂ ਗ੍ਰੰਥ ਸਾਹਿਬ : ਅੰਗ ੧੧ ਪੰ. ੧੫
Raag Asa Guru Ram Das Guru Granth Sahib Ang 11

Vaheguru (Creator) please help me to type my book.
Jan 03, 2019, 6:30pm, Columbia, MD

Introduction

When I first met Dr. Ajaib Sidhu, MD and Dr. Hema Sidhu, some 15 years ago, I was instantly impressed with the depth of love they had for each other. I also realized they were both extremely spiritual. And as time went on their love just seemed to continue to deepen. In our many conversations about our different spirituality I found my spirituality was deepening.

Dr. Ajaib Sidhu was a world-famous doctor with many international awards. Although we became good friends, I was so mesmerized by his presence that I always, even to this day, called him Dr. Sidhu.

I was honored to be with Hema at Dr. Sidhu's bedside as he was going through his final days and hours. His death was a monumental loss to all who knew him and to the world. Just imagine what a loss it was for Hema. I have been so amazed how she is and has been handling her intense and agonizing grief. Through her ordeal she has truly balanced her grief with the joy of his life. Even though Dr. Sidhu is gone in body he is and probably always will be connected to Hema in spirit. They were and are true soulmates.

This book describes her journey through the first two years of her grief following Dr. Sidhu's death. Each chapter portrays the amazing accomplishments she achieved on her journey.

By Jack Dunlavey

Chaplain, Chaplaincy Service Department, Howard County General Hospital

John Hopkins Medicine in Howard County

About the Author

Hema Kaur Sidhu, Ph.D., RPSGT, RST

Hema Kaur Sidhu has an extensive background in academics, research, and industry, in the field of Neuroscience and Sleep Medicine.

Her volunteer activities include: Pastor Volunteer at Chaplaincy Department, Howard County General Hospital, Affiliated with Johns Hopkins. She has a Chaplaincy certification for FEMA-Federal Emergency Management Agency. Active Member of Faith Leaders Response Team, Montgomery County, MD- that responds to local acts of hate, violence, and racism. Active member of All Faiths in Friendship Group (Jewish, Christian, Muslim, Sikh, Hindu, Baha'i, Mormon lay leaders). Emotional Spiritual Care Volunteer for Montgomery County, Maryland. Group Leader of Mental Health First Aid Program for the community, through Guru Nanak Foundation of America, Silver Spring, MD. Charter Member and Former President of Khalsa Toastmasters Club, Silver Spring, MD. Counsellor of the Youth Khalsa Toastmasters Gavel Club. She received Hind Ratan Award from India.

Reason for the Book

To Inspire

Sharing Presence of the Creator in

forms of Angels Among Us

Contents

Introduction 5

About the Author 7

Reason for the Book 8

Life's Approach 10

Infant Mind - Face Facts 11

Adapting the Mind in Early Stages of Grief 15

Growth of Mind in Grief 20

A Mindset to Let Go in Grief 25

Detachment 29

Glimpse 36

Chiseled Mind Born Again- My 9 Months Anniversary 38

Walks 42

Mixed Emotions 45

March 2018 50

Snowy Spring Day 52

Progression of Mind One-year April--2018 53

Challenges 60

Highlights How I Moved Forward 62

Pearls 65

Life's Approach

Oct. 03, 2018 5:30pm.

Struck by Grief: My choices were - Be a victim or Be a Conqueror

I decided to conquer the grief. I moved forward by experiencing the Creator by my side, in my thoughts and in actions.

Thanks to the Creator for sending waves of inspiring thoughts. In the process I acknowledged my loss. I experienced a roller coaster of emotions. My best expression was on paper with a pen.

There are different ways to channelize the ethereal energy flowing through you at all the times. There is something special about the grieving time. It is the time when an individual is fine tuned to discover his or her Inner self. I am blessed that I was able to connect.

Spiritual readings, wisdom of wiser people, helped me analyze each day through the process of chiseling my mind.

Infant Mind - Face Facts

On Oct. 06,2017, I was pondering over how my mind has been chiseled in the past six months. My husband Ajaib passed away on April 10, 2017. My time with him was a precious gift from the Creator.

I wanted to stay strong and lead a life he would be proud of me for. I challenged myself and tried to move forward, in an effort to maintain our regular schedule of activities. For example, I attended the Medical conference at the Baltimore Inner Harbor, which was routine practice of our team- my husband, our friend Dr. Swaroop and myself that brought back a lot of my memories.

In the month of April, a few days after his passing, I realized that my professional license was about to expire. I had to take care of this responsibility since I was far from retirement and knew I had to continue earning a living. In addition, utility bills, insurance, financial planning - mortgage, paying off loans, shredding of very old important documents- all these took a lot of my time and mental capacity. I felt like I had no choice but to keep on working and moving forward. In addition to regular tasks and paperwork, I was also in the midst of collecting supporting documents for my mother's USA permanent residency application.

The Sheep Festival at the Howard County Fairgrounds, MD, was another event which we both always used to enjoy. This time my mother accompanied me. His presence was felt on the unpaved path we used to walk on, dirt of which would cover our shoes. Our favorite stops were Popcorn stall and then Ice cream. I missed him dearly but he was still holding my hand. When coming to buying something for me from the festival our favorite place was the Alpaca booth. This year, I just passed by it, not ready to settle on a purchase.

Oh! I forgot to mention his favorite earmuffs sheep skin booth. He used to buy those and very creatively he would use them as his forehead band, as he was always cold on his forehead. I stopped at the booth, looked at the vendor. He was busy. Ajaib whispered 'it is ok'. Tears rolled down my cheeks and I moved on.

I felt as if the Creator had planned my visit to the Sheep Festival as a much needed break from the overwhelming obligatory projects around me. In May 2017- I had no choice but to work on a lot of deadlines of various projects both personal and professional. While I was working on my projects, I was supported by my friends, the lovely couple, Prakash Singh and Hardeep Kaur. The circle of my friends changed in the blink of an eye. Those I thought would be with me had become strangers. Others, who I knew were sincere, busy people, they held my hand through the journey. I was perplexed by some who distanced themselves from me. I asked myself "what did I do? Why a change in their behavior?" I could not get an answer. After trying to resolve these questions in my own mind, I approached Chaplin Jack and his words of wisdom were "that it is normal." Accepting that there was nothing I could do about it took me to the next step.

My goal of staying involved was well supported by the Creator. The Creator presented multiple back-to-back opportunities for me to be engaged in and to give back to the community. As an example, it just so happened that on a weekend in June, I had a volunteer opportunity at the hospital, a family birthday celebration, and a religious prayer of thanks to help in.

Howard County General Hospital, Columbia, MD, where I volunteer as a Pastoral visitor, selected me to participate in a disaster drill on June 4, 2017. I accepted the challenge, of participating in the drill on my own. I reflected on how we both would have been part of the drill had my husband been around. He and I had been volunteer Pastoral visitors at the hospital for 9 years. In the evening I was invited to a birthday party of the 3-year-old in my in-laws family from noon to 4pm. At 5pm on the same day I was invited to a religious ceremony of gratitude for a young lady who was starting a new job as an IT consultant. At their place we had Langar (food prepared as a community for all who attend). I stood at the stove, helping with the meal, until all 60 guests had been fed. Friends watching me expressed awe at how actively I was engaged in such activities during my time of mourning. In fact, I was doing everything by putting my mind in the PRESENT. Angels were helping me by keeping me company on different occasions, with different people in my life all on the same day.

Perpetual thought of loss, along with working on professional and personal goals, helped me initiate the process of aligning my infant mind in grief with harmony.

Adapting the Mind in Early Stages of Grief

On June 05, 2017, a new chapter of my life started unfolding. My mother's final supporting documents (which I had started collecting in May 2017) for permanent residency of USA were dropped at the USCIS office in Catonsville, MD. The documents were requested by the immigration office within a certain, strict time frame. I was able to accomplish that.

In the evening my teenaged niece made her final decision to move from California to Maryland for her studies and moved in with me. I welcomed her and bought the airline tickets. So, I had a teenager landing in my lap whom I had not had contact with for 15 years. To me she was a stranger. She is a lovely, smart young lady but needed to be guided to channel her energy and actions. I did not know what challenges she would bring in my life. I introduced her to Howard Community College, to pursue her courses. I helped her with a job at the hospital.

All the above projects with her took a lot of my time and energy. Subconsciously, I was endeavoring to accomplish the wish of my husband, as he believed in the power of togetherness of family.

Here is a remarkable moment which I would love to share for the month of July 2017. I saw my husband's eyes in my last REM cycle (dream cycle) in early AM hours. I felt weird and hushed it in my dream. But the dream was persistent. I could not make sense of it at that time. I woke up, I was led to my patio in my backyard, in a very peaceful surrounding. I was relaxing in the lawn chair. I found my niece outside doing mischief.

The intense deep thoughtful dream in which I saw the eyes of my husband, acted as the guiding light which was a visionary signal to go watch and keep an eye on my surroundings. It was my husband's strong love and my guardian angel's presence which led me to the backyard. This incident gave me strength and courage to stay strong and vigilant.

In July, I was Invited as Guest speaker at the Science of Spirituality Center in Washington, DC. My first thought was that it would be very difficult to attend without him by my side. After a brief conversation with my mind, I told myself to adapt to the change and I accepted the challenge. My husband had always been very supportive, always wanting me to share the radiance of the Creator in me. I knew he would want me to do this. My friend was kind enough to drive me to the Center. I was accompanied by my mother, niece and my friends. Having a support system around and adapting to receive help was very helpful. It was a very successful event. I'm glad that I did not keep myself from speaking at it. It helped me grow and heal just a little more.

Visiting Gurdwara in August - I visited Gurdwara (place of worship of Sikh faith) after not having attended regular services for 4 months. I used to teach a group of the young kids, between age 5 to 17 years under Nanak Spiritual academy-about the Sikh faith and how they can feel connected to themselves. After the service, I left with a heavy heart as we both were always together. As I was walking down the steps, a young Sikh boy came up to me, I had never met him before. He introduced himself and asked me if I was a Toastmaster? I was blown away. In the past I had a plan to launch a Youth Gavel Toastmasters Club. He gave me a chance to smile and have hope. The message was not to leave the Gurdwara disheartened.

The Young man's name was Jugraj Singh. He asked me if he could join the Toastmasters club. I readily agreed and told him he could come as my guest in one of the meetings. I told him about my plans of launching a Youth Gavel Toastmasters Club in Sept. 2017. His eyes lit up and he willingly said Yes to becoming a member in an exciting tone. After this incident I felt as if my guardian angel (Ajaib) was always with me – just coming in front of me in different forms and shapes.

July 4, 2017 was Independence Day and I decided to join the parade in Washington, D.C. with the group representing the Sikh community. My niece accompanied me as this was her chance to participate in a national activity and explore D.C. We had the privilege to ride in the bus with the local Sikh community members. We were part of the team. Some were carrying the banner that identified which group we were, some were walking with matching shirts, and I was handed a national flag to carry. I learnt later that the picture taken during the parade, focused on me carrying the flag, was used in media all over the world. As I was in the process of editing the script of this memoir, I linked it to the words of my husband who told me in early March 2017 that you will become a star. This incident boosted my Morale.

By the end of August my niece was settled, I was not giving her rides to college during the day and to work back and forth in the middle of night (she was on evening shift). I was relieved of that responsibility. I received a call from two parents about my plans of continuing to teach at Nanak Spiritual Academy, as the summer ended without any sessions. I decided to let go of my teaching to kids for a while. The teaching project was started by both of us. I used to teach, and he was always there in the class to support me. I felt that presenting myself to the kids in the current state of mind with unsettled vibrations from me may not be healthy for the kids. So, I decided to quit on that and told them to join classes in another basic language school.

After evaluating the state of my mind in these very early stages of Grief. I realized that I had moved forward from being a single person to having the company around me all the time. My mind accepted the change of having others around.

Growth of Mind in Grief

Now here comes the connection for my next event. I mentioned earlier that on June 04, 2017 I volunteered for a disaster hospital-based drill. There I met a young girl with her father. We started talking and I mentioned to her that she could develop her leadership skills via the Toastmasters International Club. We exchanged phone numbers and emails. Her father was very excited when I told him that I would appoint her the President of the Youth club if she could lead 15 to 20 youth. She did come up with a list of 15 teenagers under the age of 18 years. Now, with this list of future members I set forth to launch the Youth Toastmasters Gavel Club. Somewhere in my mind I knew I needed more time and I told her that I would start in September. I was dealing with emotions- sad, crying, missing my husband. What hit me the most was loss of my appetite which had been an immediate response of my body facing any intense, sad emotions.

The young future President of the Youth Gavel club was persistent, and she started sending me emails asking about the commencement date. Motivated by her enthusiasm, I gathered myself together and decided to fill out the application to start the Youth Gavel Toastmasters Club. I wanted to keep my promise to the young girl.

I did receive the final approval from the Toastmasters International Office to get started. I was able to launch the Youth Gavel Toastmasters Club on Oct.01, 2017. It was a tribute to my loving husband who was very passionate about youth activities.

In the month of October, I had to handle a lot of social/community Interfaith commitments. I challenged myself to be the Toastmasters Contest Master on Oct 4, 2017. I listened to my impulses, followed them and felt confident.

On Oct. 05, 2017. I was in a family counselling session with my friend. I got more out of the session than my friend. I got a chance to express myself. How our marriage was successful as my husband and I were intertwined. I discussed how we resolve our issues when we had differences of opinion. My husband told me one time that Marriage is like a carpenter's workshop, everyday one must work on it. The session with my friend brought back so many memories. I felt that every day I was taking little steps forward, cherishing his lovely spirit on my side.

On Oct. 8, 2017 I went for the Unity Walk in Montgomery County, helping my mind to get back on trajectory with emotional, and spiritual growth, and confidence.

On Oct. 09, 2017, I decided to commence the religious ceremony (commencement of reading holy scripture). At my place I had the company of my niece, nephew and my mother. My mind knew that

I wanted all of them to be at my wavelength, but the situation was very different- niece and nephew had their own issues- niece rushing to college and nephew had only a few minutes. I decided to stay out of their problems, the reality of the situation was very different than my perception. I wanted to cherish my own memories of my husband. I did tell all the family members that I would commence the religious ceremony in about half an hour. I prepared the offering and quietly went to the prayer room. My mother joined me, and my brother joined over the phone. I thanked my brother calling as in the last days of my husband's life he had been a big support to me. In the morning hours I was able to accomplish the commencement of the reading of the holy Scripture (Guru Granth Sahib Ji) in the memory of my husband. I was longing to connect to the essence of my being. The lesson learnt was one can be attached to one's loved ones, those who are around in the physical forms and yet also be attached to your memories.

I would like to mention that finding purpose during the period of grief is very hard, heartbreaking yet essential. In my case, the connections were revived. I met my friend Rupal Dev at a restaurant Mango Grove, Columbia, MD on Oct 06, 2017. The three of us had planned to meet after 20 years of gap. The Creator had His/Her own plan. Only two of us were able to connect. That is what was meant to be. My friend Rupal Dev and I sat there for about 3 hours catching up on 20 years since we had last met. At the end of our time together we felt the time was too short. On Oct 09, 2017, I was going for meditation hour and I invited her. After the session, we remained standing in the parking lot for about an hour and half. After I went home, I had a very strange dizzy-woozy feeling. It was exactly the time about six months ago when my husband was fading away. It was a very intense feeling – I am unable to explain the uneasiness which crept upon me. It was almost like a visitation by him and I am telling him "you cannot leave" and I tried to rest on my bed.

The angels were very busy putting me to different tasks. I am part of the Emotional Spiritual Care Team in Montgomery County, Maryland. On Oct. 23, 2017, I was invited to give a presentation on 'How to approach Sikh Faith based population in a disaster Scenario'. On Oct 25, 2017, I received a request to submit a brief article for publication in the Community Newsletter about the Youth Gavel Toastmasters Club which I had launched earlier in the month. I was constantly put to work by angels. All this was happening in addition to my professional responsibilities as I continued to work full time.

On Oct 27, 2017, I attended a family friend's son's pre-wedding party, followed by a wedding and reception. It was very hard for me to face the crowd without my husband. Sometimes, during the bereavement period, making decisions is not easy. For me, it took me about a month to decide if I should attend the ceremonies. I made my decision by constantly preparing myself for the reality and listening to my inner voice. The mind grows in Grief only if one allows it to be open to the ideas and have perception of change.

A Mindset to Let Go in Grief

Nov 19, 2017

Here and there, I do get the message that raising expectations in the period of bereavement is not a good idea. On Nov 1, 2017 I felt like I was shattered by my surroundings. This is the day I picked up my dream car in 2012, with my loving husband. On that day we had no clue how we were going to pay for it. Since it was my dream car for which I worked very hard, my husband supported me. Truly the Creator paved the path for us to accomplish our goal. Our wish was fulfilled. We received more than we asked for. I was missing his physical presence. My wish was to clean my car and enjoy the day, but it ended up being a day where I felt lonely. I was fighting my loneliness. I went to the nearby Howard Community College as I wanted to donate some of the computers and cables to the new SET (Science Engineering and Technology) department for students' hands-on training. I did go to the parking lot of the college but did not feel like going to the department and asking for the protocol of donating the items. I felt like I was frozen in the zone. My childhood friend called me, and she was online with me across seven seas while I was in the parking lot. After talking to her for a few minutes, I moved out of the college without accomplishing my goal. One thing which came to my mind was she was acting as an Angel for me. I believe it was important for me to feel the experience of being frozen. I was able to pull myself out of it. I drove to Centennial Park near my house and visited our favorite spot. I parked my car and enjoyed the serenity of the Lake. I felt his presence there and had a few moments of conversation- it was like a visitation by him.

After a while I started back home, my neighbor Linda (sincere friend and walking buddy) called me to join her for a walk, which was a blessing for me. I am lucky that I have a few lakes around my place where I live. I was able to walk around the Wild Lake and got a chance to vent my feelings to her.

On Saturday Nov 18, 2017 I had the opportunity to attend a Sikh community wedding. A lot of memories came back as there were a lot of old friends. Many of them came to give me hugs and apologize for not being in touch. I do understand the reality of life (out of sight out of mind). Each one of us gets so busy in our daily routine- hustle and bustle that we forget to give each other some precious moments in which we share the loving memories of the departed soul.

My test on this day was my niece who accompanied me to the wedding. I was testing myself if I could detach myself from her. She is a lovely young lady and has her own perception of life. She wanted to enjoy her music during 45 minutes of ride each way, and was on social media with her friends. I used to feel as though she was ignoring me with her actions, but today I was determined not to interrupt her and let her enjoy as I invited her to join me. While my husband was alive, my immediate family was not in the picture of my life as far as coming over and spending family time with us. Now after his passing, the family is in picture. It took me 48 hours to teach myself to stay centered/detached and move on with my goal. I was able to achieve my goal by staying calm and focused. I realized that accomplishing goals in difficult times with my husband around me was much easier than struggling by myself.

There is a lot to be done between my job, responsibilities at home, my social activities - which I am enjoying - all of this helps me to keep moving forward with a positive attitude. The lesson I have learned is that I do need to untangle myself from some responsibilities to be more peaceful.

The feeling of being overwhelmed knocks repeatedly in the bereavement period. Having angels close to oneself as sincere friends, always helps. One such friend has experienced a lot of ups and downs of life. On Sunday, she was kind enough to come over and spend a few hours with me to sort out my husband's things. I had attempted to do this in the past but was not able to accomplish it on my own. I feel blessed to have friends like her in my life. She kindly helped me sort through everything. My mission was accomplished!!

Detachment

Dec 7, 2017

The day finally came after emotionally struggling to "**let go**" of my husband's last Vehicle- the Van. The one he loved so dearly I vividly remember the day we purchased it. The moment he saw the van it was an AHAA!! moment for him. He got in the van posed with his hands on the steering wheel-His smile explained everything to me -comfort, ease and his classical style. The salesman was eager to show us another vehicle and my husband responded, "This is it-no need to look any further." I was happy as the exterior color was of my choice, to which he graciously agreed. The idea of buying the Van was to be able to accommodate the whole family if and when they visited. That wish was never fulfilled while he was alive. All the memories were refreshed of the time period when we purchased his Van during his birthday week – the Van was his birthday gift. We both made wonderful memories with it. Our favorite one was our longest trip to Canada. We enjoyed the road trip, driving by lakes.

Finally, after he passed away, his nephew Gurpreet who helped us a lot during his sickness, one day asked me if he could buy the Van. I was not ready to part with his Van and I said no. I guess the timing was not right since it was just one month after his passing. I was not in a state of mind where I could make rational decisions. Somehow I still wanted to hold onto it in my garage. The possible reason was that I was thinking my brother who lives in California might be able to move in with me and move to Maryland. With that hope, I gave myself a time frame of six months.

See, the point I am trying to make here is that I contradicted myself between raising my hopes and preparing myself to start a new chapter of my life. Neurologically, metaphysically somewhere I had the answer that I will have to let it go.

Six months passed and there was no sign of my brother. My niece who was a teenager did not want to drive it either. So, it was time for me to move on.

I had already lost a chance to give the Van to his nephew. So, when I was ready, I asked his nephew, who at one point was keen. He told me that he had locked in a price for another vehicle of his choice. Without prospective buyers in the family, I started with a wish that it should go to a family - who would need it and appreciate the value of it.

So, now the message was very clear that I needed to detach and be strong. With a heavy heart I started marketing- received a few cold phone calls that things did not materialize. My last resort was to take it to the CarMax dealer. I had resolved with my emotions that I will let it go by Dec 31, 2017.

On Dec 5, 2017, I had a visitation with my husband. I told him that I was feeling overwhelmed and he needed to do something and he sure did. It unfolded like this. On Dec 6, 2017 morning I received a text from the sweetest person, Hunghee that she was interested in the van. When I read the message, I knew that was the absolute right fit. With the van going to Hunghee, my husband helped me to detach from the Van and move on with life.

I met the couple Hunghee and Byungchul on Dec 7, 2017 in Columbia, MD. They both came to test drive with an offer. I was by myself and after a brief introduction, I requested that they test drive the Van in a nearby parking lot. They agreed and in less than five minutes they made the decision. They were very impressed. I opened the briefcase with papers of my Van, tears rolling down my cheeks, with any effort to hold them back in vain. The couple thought it was because of my attachment to the van. Finally, I told them it belonged to my husband. I unfolded the story that he had passed away. The couple was very compassionate—he was a Pastor, his wife a homemaker. I told them I volunteered as a Pastoral Visitor in the hospital. From that conversation, confidence started building on both sides.

We started discussing how the Creator has put us together. I found out that they had lost a similar van in summer, and ever since then they had been praying to find something similar. It was approximately the time that I made up my mind to *Let Go* of the Van. I felt that I was no longer by myself in this deal - of handing over the vehicle.

Hunghee and Byungchul helped me to store the things in my office. On our way out, we met Chaplin Jack - a great person who helped me in my journey of mind chiseling. My husband was very fond of Chaplin Jack. The whole day went like a breeze.

I consulted my friend, Hardeep, as to how I should handover the keys and tags. I was advised to bring tags with me once I give the keys. I relayed the message to the couple.

This suggestion put us, - the couple and me, in a brainstorming session. Each one of us was coming up with ideas on how to handle the situation as they did not bring a temporary tag with them. I told them that it is not me giving ideas to them but the Creator himself is acting through me.

Being a Pastor, he understood the point. Finally, the decision was made that I would ride with them to Virginia and transfer the title. During our one-hour trip to the MVA office, I shared with them the memories of the van and what it meant to me. Amidst the stories, we all were laughing, making fun of each other and marveling at how we were feeling like puppets in the hands of the Creator. They were thinking of sending me back by Uber taxi. I told them I was not comfortable riding alone in one so we considered other options. The Van transfer was completed, and they were given the Ok for the vehicle to be on the road for one full year without any additional responsibilities. We were all very thrilled.

The time was 3:30pm, they needed to pick up their little boy Sung Wee from school. For the boy, the Van was an early Christmas gift. It was time for me to head back home. The couple offered that they could drop me off at the public transport train. Inside my heart, I was thinking that was a challenge- I had never taken an Interstate train but could manage.

The whole situation took a different turn. As if they both heard me talking to my inner self. They asked me if I was hungry as they were also hungry. I said I am hungry but could manage for a few hours. They asked me if I wasn't under a time constraint, they'd like for me to visit their home and meet their son. When they mentioned about meeting their son, I thought I should go visit and see his precious smile. We all started the journey to their apartment.

Father went to pick up his son while Hunghee and I picked up food. Finally, I met Sung Wee (son) he was very excited and immediately hopped in his seat. He was overjoyed, jumping saying, "That is mine." Hunghee captured that moment in a video and shared with me. I was so relieved that it was worth waiting to find the right family who would enjoy the Van.

We all then went to the cozy little apartment. The love and warmth of the family made me feel as if I was part of their family. We all had dinner together, which was led by prayer by little Sung Woo.

I was offered Korean tea which I enjoyed and was given a demo on how to save and prepare the ingredients of the tea.

Hunghee was so kind - she gave me three small sandwich bags of dried ingredients for the tea. She also introduced me to a Korean fruit and gave me some to take home. Her generosity was unparalleled.

Now, it was time for me to start the trip back home. It was a school night and it was going to take them three hours for a round trip with little Sung Woo. They kept reassuring me that he will be fine.

In the middle of this, I received a message from my niece that she was getting off work early. I requested her to meet us in the middle and she agreed. That was the moment for me that I was truly not alone. My angel, my husband, was with me. It was as if the Creator was walking along my side. The presence of the Creator was so intensely felt throughout the day that it's hard to put the profound experience in writing.

The transition from Let go, to detachment, to compassion, to warmth, to love which I received from the family was like a happy ending.

I conclude by this – no matter how difficult the task is when you are making decisions on your own- truly believe in yourself, be with the soulmate, appreciate the metaphysical bond and the Creator leads you. Have faith- new members of Universal family come and meet you and help make new memories.

I wished the Vehicle would go to someone who needed it and would enjoy it. My wish came true.

Glimpse

Jan 15, 2018

Life keeps changing every day, every hour, every second. The challenge is How I was doing in that moment which is transitory and bid goodbye in the blink of an eye. Well, every moment is a new life now without my soulmate. How precious were those golden moments we had together—SIGH!!!

My New Year's Eve, my new year day were all very different. We had rituals of either going out to a place of worship or spending time together watching the New York City ball drop at midnight. To be the first one to wish Happy New Year to each other… all that was missing this Year 2018—It was very quiet, my mother who was with me at that time had gone to bed early. So, it was just me watching the New York ball drop, welcoming 2018 by myself and of course he was smiling at me and was saying "you will be fine." The warmth of his hugs and gentle whispering were still felt and heard. He was watching every step I take, when I stumble, he cautions me to be careful.

I had been closely observing myself. I am mindful of myself-self-evaluation. I tried to be gentle as my hurt was very Deep. It may appear that the outer layer of my cells is doing fine but the nerve endings supplying them are sending emotional pain signals which clogged the flow of actions and reactions for a while. I did find myself forgetful in my own world of thoughts, feeling his companionship, his imaginary body around me. Little things which I forget- looking for glasses when I had them on my head rather than eyes. I am pretty sure many can relate to this even under normal circumstances, but for me it started after he passed away. I took this forgetful mind along to the next level of realization, where I could see myself moving forward while all other family members are walking on their paths of life. I found my path is distinct.

Chiseled Mind Born Again
My 9 Months Anniversary

I attended my All Faiths in Friendship Group Book meeting on Jan 10, 2018. For the first time I was able to share with the sisters of All Faiths how I felt to host the meeting in April 2018. (April 10, 2017 was the day he passed away). As the anniversary was approaching fast, I was lucky that I was given the time to speak. They are all very good listeners, and very supportive and encouraging. On the same day, I happened to be sitting and watching a talk show on an international channel in my native language, while sipping on my evening tea, which was our routine around 3pm. There was a young woman who was interviewed about her passion for the Sikh community (I am a Sikh faith follower). The conversation moved me to provide contributions as well. I picked up the phone and provided my inputs to the conversation in the Live talk show. I was "On Air" WOW WOW!! I did not know from where the power came and boosted me to share my thoughts. I managed to record myself. Later, I was able to rewind and listen to my opinion and my thoughts that I had shared with the young lady. To my surprise, - I did a pretty good job. There were a few things which I mentioned while I was "on Air." They were that 1.) I was invited as a speaker in March 2016 at the National Cathedral in Washington, D.C. 2.) In Oct. 2017, I launched Youth Khalsa Toastmasters International Gavel Club for Under 18 kids. 3.) Launching of Mental Health First Aid team. I felt like I bragged about myself. Then guess who whispered – Dr. Ajaib—"You did the right thing. This is what I have been telling you to do. You have all this talent, potential, you are dynamic and the world needs people like you". I finally let those words of wisdom sink in. To me, I was going through a day of mixed emotions. I felt that I did a pretty good job marking the 9 month anniversary.

This was almost like a turning point for me. I felt that I was ready to face a change—a statement which was quite challenging. Thoughts crossed my mind. There was still so much to do-emotionally, physically—with his belongings. He was an incredible man with so much involvement in different spheres of life—photography, writing, medical profession-up to date- Tip Top (we all know it requires maintenance-Laughing Out Loud). How could I part with all that?? Such loving and fond memories, those moments when he was capturing nature, the ink from his pen would just flow with his thoughts and I would be with him witnessing all that—how Precious!!

How I was dealing with all this is "The Question". I found that in the past nine months I had been staging my emotions. The best I could describe is that when one puts a house on sale – my real estate friend uses the term *staging*.

It was this type of staging that was happening in my life. I had been taking a phased approach with his belongings, staging the phases along the way. I moved some of his clothes from one room to another for a couple of months, followed by taking them off the hangers, then folded in a closet shelf for a while and then finally boxed for donation. I packed some for family friends who were willing to enjoy some of his belongings.

I did the same staging with one of his favorite recliners - which we both agreed to part with before his passing, but it never did.

To me, being sensitive to the emotional barrier is very important. It is hard when you are making decisions on your own - command center of the brain - one part of the brain tells you to act, and the other part of the brain stops by saying you cannot do it. There is a very delicate balance between the two. Knowing well that one day everybody eventually parts with the belongings of loved ones. I am privileged to take all the time –to go through his belongings, stage them and finally part with them—as I am blessed with space.

I do think about those who are underprivileged. Do they hold on?? Can they hold on?? These questions help me to understand my process from a different perspective. These thoughts were showing me GLIMPSES of my future. These thoughts were provoking me to look forward, untangle from the materialistic things.

Walks

Jan.20, 2018, 1:40pm

Every day walk—Being a wife of a physician-walking, changing the environment, daydreaming was like a routine of our lives. My husband would make sure that I went out for a daily walk. It could be with him if his schedule permitted or with my loving neighbor Linda with our four-legged wonderful spirit –Tiger (Linda's dog) or just myself.

I am very blessed to have Lakes around my house, which are within walking distance. I have lots of memories with him going to the different lakes nearby, posing with geese, bald eagles flying, birds chirping and squirrels dancing. Some of the spots became our favorite spots to sit and enjoy serenity.

I will share a story. My husband went through a joint replacement and was undergoing home physical therapy. He was unable to go for a walk with me. I was not in a mood to go for a walk. He insisted that I should keep myself healthy no matter what. He knew it was important for my sanity. My friend, Linda, and Tiger came. He told me to go for a walk with them. I asked him how long he thought I should go for a walk. He smiled and said, "When you see three squirrels then turn back." Linda, Tiger and I went for a walk. To my surprise I saw three squirrels dancing around the tree and Linda witnessed it—we both laughed and came back home. He was truly an amazing man. On my return, I told him the story of squirrels, he smiled and said, "I told you I would be fine, and you would feel good after the walk." I have lots of stories like that.

I have a pretty WOW!! Story to share after he passed away. As routine started to build up, I went out for a walk with Linda and Tiger. This time it was in the neighborhood around the block. Since it had been raining very heavily, we decided to stay away from the path which was through the woods to the lake as it was flooded. I must admit that I was feeling low that evening. I was very quiet while walking. Linda was showing me the clouds and it was almost dusk. I looked up and to my surprise I saw the clouds with sun peeking, making a sort of necklace of pearls. During this I saw a cloud shaped like Dr. Ajaib's turban with his long face, well-groomed beard (he was a follower of Sikh faith), as if he was looking down and smiling. I was blown away. I stood there for a moment and told Linda to look up. She looked at it and then asked me, "Are you seeing what I am seeing?" I responded, "Yes"—which was Dr. Ajaib smiling at us. Linda said sure "he is watching you." She said he "wanted" you to be happy. That day I wanted to capture the scene. Certain moments are not meant to be captured but to retain as memories---I was not carrying my cell phone with me. The glimpse of the above is on the cover page.

I guess the Superpower/Creator/GOD wants me to hold on to faith. Walking 3 to 4 days a week with Linda and Tiger gave me moments to heal. These walks became therapeutic for me. I was able to vent as Linda is a very patient listener. She also loved Dr. Ajaib and always admired him. So, it was easy for me to relate to her. I joked with Linda that I chew her ears by repeating my stories, sharing my memories—which I have learned is part of my bereavement period.

Mixed Emotions

Feb 18, 2018

February happened to be the month filled with events for both of us and my family. It is the tenth month into the bereavement period. I am blessed! I am blessed! Every breath is precious. I wonder how many times I had been saved from falling back in the emotional ditch. Thank you, Creator, for creating the opportunities which came to me and the Creator had put me on the front to be His Conduit.

No wonder my husband used to say that I am amazing, lovely, dynamic, vibrant—over and over. I guess he truly understood the plane of our energy where we were both operating. Ever since he has left his physical form, there have been challenges in my life, one may call it distraction, an opportunity, company to keep myself occupied. These were opportunities for me to feel that I am a conduit –our role in the lives of people is not over yet. My husband helped me to build the base for the community and family to build on.

When I reflect on the last ten months, I see how many precious opportunities came to me to act in a positive way, to pave the path for all those who met me from far away. Relationships that were almost lost were revived. The dreams of anybody young, middle aged, old – were witnessed being fulfilled. The most distinct memory was my neighbor sitting in the lawn helpless. He had a heart attack while he was walking around the block. I happened to be in the driveway and was called for help. I guess I was called for, to be Tested by the Creator. I had thought I was going for a meeting. Instead, here I was in a situation where I found my neighbor in a life-threatening situation. I attended to the neighbor, initiated 911 and he was taken to the hospital. Later I found out that he had surgery and was doing fine. On another instance, I was able to help my brother initiate his immigration application which he had been postponing for 2 years. What an opportunity to help. The Creator is Great!! Thank you Creator! I think I "passed."

Jan. 22, 2018 to Feb 09, 2018 had been a very busy time among us: mother, brother, niece and me. My mother stayed with me from Oct. 2016 to Feb 2018. It was time for her break. So, I planned a trip for her to go to India on Feb 9, 2018. A farewell environment was created for days. All the friends who loved my mother came to see her. Every day the house was full of people. In the midst of that, I wanted to complete the reading of the holy Granth (Scripture of SIKHS - word Guru) in loving memory of my father who passed away on Feb 16, 2015. My mother thought it was too much for me to handle. I was confident that I could accomplish it with divine force by my side. By HIS grace the mission was accomplished.

Everything went according to plan on Feb 8, 2018 with family together via physical presence and via Video.

On Feb 9, 2018, it was the day my mother was travelling to India- a long international flight. She is very lucky as her two children- brother and me and her grand-daughter were present to take her to the airport. She got a VVIP treatment at the airport, as she was considered a *family friend.* My husband's nephew works at the airport. After she boarded the plane, my brother and niece also left for their work. I had a few hours by myself before my niece returned from work. So, with all this a new chapter of life began for me.

Feb 11, 2018, was our anniversary. I had planned to relax and spend time by myself, but the Creator intervened. However, to my surprise, I received a call from an old friend of mine that a young person from our group passed away. I felt obliged and did not want to miss the final prayers ceremony. This was in addition to my previously planned engagements. The day was filled with mixed emotions—I am Vice President of education for adult Toastmasters Club and counsellor for Youth Gavel club. So, I had to attend both meetings. Youth members were excited as they were giving their prepared speeches. I had no choice but to attend. After both the meetings were over, I attended the final prayers of my friend. This was not the way I wanted to spend our anniversary without my husband physically present. On my way back home after a long day, I decided to drive to the bakery from where we used to pick up our cake. I was driving, it was dusk and so the emotions were pounding. I felt a tsunami of tear's at the verge of my tear's glands. I was driving, and as memories were consuming my mind, I passed the bakery and landed on the wrong road.

When I realized that I was on the wrong road, I decided to head back home without the cake. The next moment I saw a new sign of a Pastry shop in that area. I decided to check it out. From the moment I parked, to stepping in the pastry shop, it was very difficult. This was the first time being myself to buy a cake. It took me a while to order. I did buy the cake and came home. I thought I would share it with my niece who was living with me, but then I realized that she was in her own world and was not in tune with me. I ended up enjoying the cake myself. As the time was passing, it was becoming harder and harder. I decided to pull our album out and refreshed my memories. With God's Grace I survived.

My next challenge was Valentine's day which was also my husband's birthday. We had a routine of getting massages between our anniversary and his birthday. I called our massage therapist, I had to break the news to her that this year it was just me. I called her very late to book the appointment. I knew I would not be able to get it on the day I wanted, but I did make the appointment for later in the month. The next day, I was lucky to get the spot – my therapist somehow managed to accommodate me. So, I decided to go in. I could not hold back my emotions—I stepped on the table and tears were all over me as it was the same room, environment – the only person missing was him. Here I was trying to move forward but- with lots of memories, I did not know how I could get over this feeling of being alone. In the evening I pulled out our favorite lights, hung them and enjoyed them by myself. As facing the days of mixed emotions gave me strength – acceptance was becoming more within reach.

March 2018

M-Meticulous, A-Adorable, R-Respectable, C-Charming, H-Honest

In March this year 2018 I was marching alone in physical form with my invisible soulmate who was meticulous about doing things big or small. I missed him sitting on his favorite recliner watching his CNBC channel, guiding me on how to manage stocks and bonds (in which I had least interest). Later I realized that he knew what difficulties I would be facing, and he was preparing me. He finally found an easy way. He gave me a session before he left his physical form. Filing taxes was one of those. The day I had an appointment to file my taxes with my accountant it happened to be the same day in 2017 when our taxes were filed while he was in the hospital. This year our taxes were to be filed jointly. It was very painful.

I requested my friend to accompany me. It was the first time that I was driving with all the paperwork. The commute itself overwhelmed me, my adorable respectable man was not physically with me. I was lucky that my friend is a patient listener, which made my process easier as I had the opportunity to express my feelings.

I prepared all my bookkeeping records in red ink - the reason was that I was hurting. I gracefully accepted the reason. Writing in red helped me to connect to the pain I had been going through every time I was thinking of putting the paperwork together for taxes.

This year 2018 was the first time in the last 15 years with the same accountant that I took two unopened letters with me. My accountant looked at me with surprise and stated "letters are unopened." I feebly replied I was aware and gave her the permission to open them. My mind was not willing to open any more letters related to our taxes. I was giving my mind a chance to go in the direction which would bring peace. Honestly, I broke down after my tax filing process was completed. I could not stop crying. My friend gently patted on my back and said, "Be strong. let's go home." In the back of my mind, I was trying to move forward, leaving old memories of 15 years of time in that office. It was a very difficult evening. In March, tax time was the biggest challenge and by God's Grace I was able to handle it.

Snowy Spring Day

There comes my birthday- according to the lunar calendar. My husband celebrated this day, making it even more special with surprises like homemade breakfast, lunch at my favorite place, and surprise dinners. Balloons, cards, hidden smiles, sometimes expressions that he forgot about it. This year there was a blanket of snow. It seems he celebrated it in a unique way with mother nature. In perfect sense that is what we used to enjoy- beauty, peace, serenity. I felt like he hugged me. There were no flowers, nobody to take me out, no mischievous smiles, surprises. It was very quiet. I was thinking a week prior to this day, that I will spend the day by myself.

After all, there was a surprise - there was Snow in Spring! What better surprise, smile could I have asked for?! He made it very SPECIAL!!

In this world, with social media, many friends sent me wishes, but it was very different. Somewhere deep down I was missing him a lot. This day my niece and brother were with me. The creator had them around me, but they both were busy with their own agenda.

Progression of Mind One-year April--2018

Missing A-Amazing P-Peaceful R-Radiant I-Intelligent L-Loving Soulmate that makes APRIL

Marching forward, I embraced April. I wanted to make it a month of tributes to my amazing, peaceful, radiant, intelligent and lovable husband. My first tribute on April 4, 2018, was when I went to Washington D.C. to participate in the A.C.T. rally to mark the 50th anniversary of Dr. Martin Luther King's assassination day. I was invited to participate in the Interfaith Prayer service which was held in the early hours of 8 am. I represented Sikhs with another Sikh, Dr. Rajwant Singh, who happened to have been mentored by my husband. It was amazing that his wish was that one day, people from Sikh faith would participate in activities like the A.C.T. rally. His wish came true on April 4, 2018. I participated to honor his wish.

Here is how I managed to get to Washington, D.C. This time I missed him a lot. All these years I felt that it would be difficult to be in Washington, D.C. on my own. He was very good at driving around in DC but for me it was a big challenge. So, my mind started thinking about how I could get there safely. I did so much brainstorming about places to park, hotel vs. place of worship, or taking Metro/train. I finally thought of my friend who works in

Washington, D.C. and approached him. How it unfolded for me was amazing. He told me that they had a carpool system and it was his turn to drive. One of his co-workers was on vacation, so it would not be an issue for him to give me a ride. I was so thankful. So, going to Washington, D.C. was resolved. I went to the stage with Dr. Rajwant Singh, offered the prayer and we were escorted to the seating area. When we were approached by the media in the seating area for brief interviews, I could feel the presence of Dr. Ajaib throughout the time I was in the ACT rally function. My friends from different faiths, after offering the prayers, slowly started to leave. Here, I was not sure how I would get back home as I did not have a ride back home.

I started talking to my mind- there were two options: one was to cling with other friends who were leaving or by taking public transport and challenge myself to reach home. I was very hesitant to take the train back home. It had been a very long time (22 years) since I had boarded the Metro/train. On March 18, 2018, I was in Washington, D.C. with my friend visiting the National Museum of African American History and Culture. My friend was very kind, as she helped me to get a travel pass for Metro, so I could travel by myself.

Now, my mind kept playing games with me "go with someone or go back home alone." After a few debates within myself, I decided that I would try to go home by myself. So, I started out confidently from the seating area. My plan was to ask the security guard and follow his directions to the Metro station. Here I approached the guard very respectfully. I asked him if he could point me towards the direction of the metro station. He replied sorry as he was not from the area. My mind said O.K. and I started my journey. I started looking around and finally found the spot. This first experience at the metro station had a funny part – the escalators were out of order and passengers were on both escalators going in both directions. I stood on the side watching passengers to figure out in which direction I should be moving. After 2 or 3 minutes, I found a family whom I think we're in the same state of mind- not sure which way to go. I observed them for a while and the next thing I know, we were all standing in the same corner. Finally, I saw a few people going down and they seemed to be Washingtonians, (I could tell from their body language- business attire, laptop bags on shoulder or in hand, walking at a fast pace towards a known destination). I decided to follow them to the underground train station. Here comes- how a naive person walks confidently. I took my Metro pass out and I tried to scan it, but it would not open the gate for me. I attempted in two different lanes and failed. I approached the Help booth and inquired why my card was not working. The officer gently pointed me to the correct lane and gave me instructions how to get to the destination station. Once I boarded the train, I called my friends – the one who gave me the ride into DC and the other who helped me get the Metro pass as both were aware that I was not feeling confident to take public transportation. I shared with them that I had accomplished boarding the right train and I was reassured by them. So, this was my roundtrip from home to Washington D.C. without my husband. It was challenging but felt good that I had achieved two things—participated in the prayer services and took the public transport travelling challenge. I felt my husband's presence through and through.

My second tribute was on April 7, 2018. Plan to commemorate. For that I started the preparations a week before, called my friends and family, and shared my plans. All the well-wishers were very enthusiastic. I faced the challenge in this process. I taught my mind a lot. There is a saying that everything happens for a reason. I had a teenager (niece) in my house who was least concerned about the preparations and did not participate to the extent that she did not even stay for the final day of the service. I was very hurt. The Creator had His own ways to help me. I met a beautiful, loving, caring niece of my friend who was about 21 years old who helped me in little things and fondly, we made memories together. So, my mind which was hurt by my niece was healed by the tender loving care of this young lady. As I was preparing the house to have a get together the weather was becoming unpredictable. Some friends were calling and checking if I was planning to postpone the event.

My mind was so absorbed in the event planning that I was not paying attention to the weather channel.

In my mind I was so confident that the weather was going to cooperate. The reason behind that is that I had a visitation from my husband, and we discussed. The final words were that everything will be fine.

On April 7, 2018, I had an open invitation to my family and friends from 11am to 3pm. I wanted to have a prayer service for an hour and then have the family/ friends enjoy the meal/snack whenever they could come and spend some time with me. I had about 50 to 60 people going in/out at my place. Everybody left their loving and caring vibrations behind which I enjoyed.

On April 9, 2018 I stayed up late. That was the day when my husband took his last breath. The way I spent my day was I dropped my brother off at his work, and went to buy a token of appreciation for the young lady who helped me a lot on April 7, 2018. After going to two different stores looking for what she might like, I felt exhausted, lost interest and drove back home. When I reached back home, I thought this had never happened to me before- lost "interest in shopping?" Then I realized that my mind was not ready for it and needed more time.

I did not feel like working during the day. I work flexible hours with a coworker. I feel I am blessed. I worked late evening hours.

As I was working on my computer the entire scene of the hospital started replaying in my mind. It was very painful. I was all by myself -in a way it was good.

On April 10, 2018 I was not sure how I would handle the day. By the Creator's Grace I had a blessed day. My friend Linda surprised me with flowers from her garden and took me out for a walk. I worked for a while on my computer. I thought about spending time with Chaplain Jack if he was around. To my surprise Chaplain Jack and Susan (Secretary) both came with beautiful flowers. They both kept me company, we fondly remembered my husband. My cleaning service personnel came to help put the house back in order.

Finally, Linda came to check on me and we both went for a walk.

I wanted to conclude my final chapter today as I mark the anniversary. This is my last story of my year long journey without my soulmate, how I faced certain challenges and how I tackled them.

One thing I have learned: Mind chiseling in grief is not easy. Yet acceptance of loss, reaching out to friends for help even for little things, allowing others to suggest help in making decisions, listening to advice all have their place. One may or may not take it or agree at that moment when it is offered. The ways my mind worked during this year of grieving – in the first six months my mind was not tuning in with the advice, but then I found myself accepting as I started involving myself in my activities. Challenging myself at times, sometimes I had to stretch myself to achieve my goals.

I did not take sedatives. Insomnia became an issue. In the initial stages of the emotional trauma all the scenes of his last days in the hospital were continually running in my mind like a film. I thought living through it was healthier for me than taking a sedative. A year later, on occasions, I do take Melatonin as it helps one sleep well. Easier said than done.

Challenges

Under normal circumstances tax times are stressful. This year 2018 I had to take care of our taxes. I started receiving the supporting documents instead of opening them immediately. I started putting them aside in a bin. For about three weeks I was looking at the bin everyday but did not feel like opening the letters. Every time I thought of opening the letters there was a barrier between my letter opener and the letters. On Feb. 18, 2018 I challenged myself to start working on it. I had to retrain my brain to finish the project of my taxes. Finally, I started communicating with my husband that this is not easy. His spirit responded “go slow, you can do it”. So, I planned to do it step by step. The next day I promised myself to just open the letters and label them. I was able to achieve it. The following day, I made a list of items that I would need for tax returns- that is all I could do that day. Then came a day to set up my scanner and computer and I called my CPA and financial advisor for support. The reason why I called them was that somewhere my little inner voice was telling me to speak up and ask for help. Just by calling my CPA and financial advisor, I was able to initiate the process of reviewing the supporting documents.

For about a month, I did not change the sheets on our bed that was the last set on which he slept. The idea was giving time to part with memories, like I shared - for me it was healthy at that time.

I took the wedding ring off and slipped it on the next finger. I could not part with the small emotion of moving the ring off. I put it back on my ring finger. It helped me, Ironically, as time passed the ring became tight and created skin irritation, and I had no choice but to take it off. After about a week when the rash settled, I was able to decide to put it back on the ring finger or move it to another. I acknowledged every little precise sign where the Creator was helping me to move forward. To me, the ring getting tight, developing irritation and then resolving all seems like the plan of the Creator.

Filling out legal forms and checking the box - Widow - heartbreaking.

Swapping his closet from one room to another, packing in boxes and finding donating closets than donating to goodwill store.

Highlights How I Moved Forward

When we start connecting to our responsibilities—we should follow our inner voice in grief. That is the BEST friend.

Setting a goal — who is setting? — I did at several occasions throughout the year—The most challenging was to be in front of the public as a speaker. In my case I was Toastmasters International Contest Master on Oct 4, 2017.

I Sought help, Meetings with Chaplin Jack Dunleavy. Resuming activities -My professional responsibilities. In addition, I started attending All Faith Women's Book Group, Interfaith activities, Pastoral Volunteering at the hospital.

In summer time Friday night movies at the Lake. While I helped myself, I was feeling his presence. I would like to share a profound incident. I went to watch a movie with my friend Barbara who is older and wiser than me. She put her hand on my head and I felt as if he touched me at that moment—This is feeling the presence of the Angels in times of one's bereavement.

Pearls

Keeping the mind open and allowing the acceptance of grief moments to touch you from time to time helps to explore, grow and move on. I have a Bracelet- it is my last gift from him. I still always wear it especially when I go out for a special meeting. The bracelet gave me a kind of support that he was with me.

Keep Self Evaluation Journal of the stages of grief.

Give yourself time to recover. Do not rush. Reading hymns, meditating (not necessarily sitting in a quiet place- it can be done anytime/anywhere) -… things do fall in place.

The Creator makes plans for all of us. I simply pray - *Guide me to the next step of my journey; Make me humble and acceptable to HIS plans.*

Who was Ajaib? A physician, lover, kind, passionate, intellectual, spiritual, full of wisdom. When he spoke, everybody paid attention to him. What I Miss the most – he was well organized- clothes, paper, data files. He was a Giver. His wish was to be known as a "Sikh Statesman." He signed off on April 10, 2017.

I would like to express gratitude to all the family and friends, those who acted as my angels.

END

Made in the USA
Middletown, DE
05 January 2021